the official guide to COUNTRY DANCE STEPS

the official guide to COUNTRY DANCE STEPS

Tony Leisner

Book Design and Production: **MacDonald Graphics**
Photography: **Patrick K. Snook**
Manuscript Preparation: **Christine Benton**
Typography: **Hagle**

Special thanks to the staff of the Pasadena Public Library,
Pasadena, Texas.

THE OFFICIAL GUIDE TO COUNTRY DANCE STEPS

Published by Chartwell Books, Inc.
A Division of Book Sales Inc.
110 Enterprise Avenue
Secaucus, New Jersey 07094

1 2 3 4 5 6 7 8 9 10

Manufactured in the United States of America

Library of Congress Cataloging in Publication Data

Leisner, Tony.
The official guide to country dance steps.

Includes index.
1. Country-dance. I. Title. II. Title: Country
dance steps.
GV1763.L373 793.3 79-67001
ISBN 0–89009–331–8

CONTENTS

INTRODUCTION

The idea for a book about country dancing (or kicker dancing as it is called in Texas) began in the Sam Houston Bookstore in the Galleria, a posh shopping mall in one of the best sections of Houston, Texas. As writers are fond of doing, I was browsing through the books, fascinated by the subjects others write about. The young clerk at the counter had little to do that evening, and when I identified myself as a writer/publisher, she looked at my new Dan Post boots and blurted out, "You should write a book on kicker dancing." She informed me that there was nothing in print, a fact I verified easily when I started to research the subject. All my life, I've been fascinated by the Old West, the cowboys and their garb, so I jumped in with both feet and hot-footed it to Gilley's, the mecca of kicker dancing. While I was there, Sherwood Cryer, the proprietor, the band, and all the employees made me feel so welcome that it made me feel like I'd always been a regular. Real country people are like that.

The rest you can read for yourself—the people in most of the pictures are from Gilley's, all of the instructional photos were taken there, as well as some of the others. So now for the first time in at least forty years there is a book on kicker dancing. To the young lady at the Sam Houston Bookstore—thanks.

This book is dedicated to Peggy Wright, Gator Conley, the Pasadena, Texas Public Library, Art Plotnik, Preis-Grossman Studio, Sherwood Cryer, and my wife, Elaine, who made this book a reality.

CHAPTER 1

TO SET THE SCENE

It is probably no surprise to anyone who tunes into any of today's news media that the world of country music and dancing—plus country clothes, country speech, and country culture in general—is finally coming into its own. After moving through the folklore and folk music-oriented 1960s into the disco-driven '70s, Americans are finding their way back to the simple and straightforward ways that characterize the good old west. Many of those who count themselves among the legions of the new country army are, of course, western or c&w fans from way back. But as the '80s come upon us, die-hard fans of every other conceivable form of music and dancing are drifting toward rockabilly, southern mountain rock, bluegrass, and even the twangy country ballads sung by country greats like Dolly Parton and Loretta Lynn.

The great strength of this trend is evidenced by the increasing frequency with which things country appear on TV and radio broadcasts, in films, in newspapers and magazines, on jukeboxes, and in the everyday doings of the average American. In short, that down-home country flavor has infiltrated our modern urban world on every level. And it seems that media leaders have been right on target in giving their audiences a deeper and longer look at that combination of old west and new that has given rise to the urban cowboy. In approximately 70 million American homes, at least one family member became glued to the TV set to watch the Country Music Association Awards broadcast in October 1979. Some sources estimate that as many as 100 million people consider themselves country music fans, though that figure probably includes the marginal fans as well as the true fanatics. Experts say that country music alone has become a 500-million-dollar industry, and the print media have followed the trail of dollar bills with publication of more than a hundred magazines that are devoted to the subject of country music and songs.

The top three magazines in the field boast a total of 400,000 subscribers, with the top periodical, *Country Music,* alone attracting 200,000 subscribers. In addition to the plethora of print on country music and dance, just about every state is home to at least one country-oriented association. Besides the large Nashville-based Country Music Association and its rival on the west coast, the Academy of Country Music, a wealth of state organizations can be found, in addition to a number of internationally-based country associations. Within the U.S., these groups range as widely in area as the Bluegrass Club in New York, the Country Music Foundation of Colorado, the Ohio Country & Western Music Association, and the Mississippi Valley Country & Western Music Association. Our northern neighbors offer the Academy of Country Music Entertainment, based in Ontario. Overseas, country music fans can find organized compatriots in Australia, England, Germany, and Sweden, among other nations.

Sociology and pop culture experts see this picture as a sign of our times. Considering the complexities and plastic trappings of modern urban cultures, the lure of the great American cowboy, the western pioneer, and the hardy and straightforward country folk in general is not difficult to understand. The basic behavior dictated by the legendary cowboy code is quite appealing to those who are tired of discussing "relationships," "self-fulfillment," and anxiety attacks, and to those who are tired of examining the world situation, today's lack of morals, and an ever-increasing crime rate.

Other contributions to the rise in popularity of country music and dancing include a renewed focus on dancing, a new respect for the wide open spaces and those who lived there, and the increasingly fuzzy dividing line between country music and pop music. Of course, the country and western type of dances taught in this book are for the most part merely new versions of traditional dances, and fiddlers still strike up many of the tunes that pioneers and farmers danced to during the 19th century. This all adds up to a combination of old and new that is appealing in both its classical simplicity and its refreshing modernity.

At dance halls and cowboy clubs like Gilley's Club of Pasadena, Texas, the industrial worker who lives in the shadow of a big city like Houston but yearns for the small-town atmosphere of the old west, urban cowboys and cowgirls can enjoy all the simple and often boisterous pleasures of the original cowboy with the freedom of the 20th century. Here, no one has any trouble telling the men from the girls (and they do mean *girls*); one needs little more than a lot of energy to dance adequately; everyone drinks as much as he wants; and anyone can go home with anyone he or she pleases.

Country dancing or cowboy dancing is becoming as popular a form of recreation today as disco during the early 1970s. At spots like Gilley's and its newer counterparts across the country, folks of all ages can be seen doing the Cotton-Eyed Joe. Besides middle-class working people, country dance has attracted members of the "beautiful people" set as well as noted celebrities like John Travolta and Marilu Henner, among others.

It is important to realize that country dance serves as an umbrella for a wide variety of folk and western dances that have evolved in the U.S. over a couple of centuries. From the California swing style to the honky tonk numbers done around Houston, and even from an individual club's style to that of another, urban cowboys of

The Bayou City Beats, the house band at Gilley's Club in Pasadena, Texas, plays to huge crowds nightly.

all persuasions are finding their own niches in the western dance world. Not only will you find a variety of dance styles used, but also a great diversity of names applied to them. One dance, or even a single step, will be called one thing in one city or club, and a completely different thing elsewhere.

Even the term "country dance," as used here, is only one of many used to denote the same basic type of dancing. Country dance also has been and is called cowboy

Longtime companion of John Travolta, star of *Urban Cowboy,* Marilu Henner shares Travolta's enthusiasm for things western. Here, she tries on some star-spangled boots.
(Courtesy Preis-Grossman)

dancing, or kicker dancing in Texas, western dancing, c&w, and a few others. Basically, they all refer to a general style that harks back to traditional Americanized folk dances, with a little of each taken from square dancing, reels, clogging, round dances, line dances, and even the contra dances of New England.

Regardless of the location or the particular name, country dance is lively and sometimes exhausting. Rumor has it that John Travolta, in preparation for his starring role in the movie *Urban Cowboy,* worked out for a full fourteen hours a day to achieve the correct country style. The flavor of country dance, along with many of the actual steps, is influenced in great measure by the attire worn by urban cowboys and cowgirls. Decked out in cowboy boots, hats, and jeans, these western swingers tend to use a smooth, flat-footed shuffle-and-glide motion in their dances. In addition, hops and kicks are included in a high percentage of the dances.

The good news for the newcomer is that, except for the subtleties in taking on that down-home air, just about anyone can learn to be a kicker-dancer in short order. The basic dance steps are all quite simple, involving no acrobatics that smack of disco or fancy ballroom dancing, and little exaggeration of personal input. In general, as long as urban cowboys and cowgirls don't give away too much of their city-slicker upbringing, they're likely to fit into some of the most country of country dance halls.

Begin your country education by reading chapter 2, which will give you a brief look at dance and sociological trends that paved the way for this new fad, as well as a dip into the myth that has always surrounded the real American cowboy.

Chapters 3 and 4 will introduce you to the great western dance halls—focusing on that be-all, end-all honky tonk, Gilley's—and the music and musicians that make cowboys and cowgirls hit the dance floor with the fervor of stampeding cattle.

Use some of the tips included in chapter 5 to deck yourself out in a country outfit any Texan would be proud of. Here you'll learn about the clothes that the original cowboys wore and how today's urban imitations have adapted this apparel to non-cowboy use.

Finally, put on your boots and try out the seven simple dances in chapter 6. Step-by-step instructions and photos help you get out there and kick up a storm as if you had been doing it all your life.

(Courtesy of the El Paso Convention and Visitors

CHAPTER 2

THE LEGEND OF THE URBAN COWBOY: A HISTORY

Throughout history, the type of dance styles adopted by various peoples has been greatly influenced by the culture, customs, and mores of the area and age they lived in. In fact, a look at the dance history of a particular country, for example, is very likely to provide an accurate reflection of not only political, economic, and cultural attitudes of the age, but also the sociological subtleties that govern everyday behavior. The strict attention paid to etiquette, fashion, and royal flourishes was certainly borne out by the dance styles of the 17th– and 18th–century courts of Europe. At the same time, the less-than-promising lot of the peasants of that same era was reflected in the informal, flourish-free steps of their folk dances.

Further, dance styles even provided a vehicle for changing times and customs. Jitterbug and later rock and roll, for examples, demonstrated young people's rebellion against restrictive customs they no longer wanted to accept. And disco dancing has been seen as a rebellion against the dull nine-to-five routines followed by many urban Americans today.

In this respect, country dancing is no exception to the rule. It is a mixture of old and new that reflects the nature of our time, and its fast-spreading popularity only proves that what country dance offers, Americans like. As such, it can be seen as another part of the cycle of events controlling not only dance history, but sociological history as well. In the specific case of the cowboy dancing covered in this book, this includes the evolution of folk/country dance and the important place in history held by the American cowboy.

A History of Country Dance

As varied as the people of this vast land called America are the dances we attribute to its name. In actuality, no truly American folk or country dances exist in their pure form today because even the American Indians' dances have been modernized and revised so that they no longer bear great resemblance to those done a few hundred years ago. Among primitive peoples of the past and present, dances were performed for the pleasure of the gods, to ensure a healthy harvest, or to heal the sick. In addition, among all peoples, dance has played a part in waging war or celebrating a war victory, at weddings and funerals, and in holiday or religious rites.

At various points in our history, dance has been banned by churches, outlawed by civil authorities, promoted by high schools, and lauded by artists and athletes. It has been as formal as a minuet in a king's court and as informal as an impromptu street-corner shuffle. Dance in the U.S. has undergone the same type of change in attitude, and the melting pot that is America has brought together all of the customs, traditions, and styles of dance that the world has to offer. Perhaps it is more accurate to say that a dance has become Americanized than that it is an American dance.

An important factor in the evolution of folk or country dance as opposed to the formal court dances—what we might today call the difference between formal, urban ballroom dancing and rural dancing—is that country dance has always been subject to a great deal of regional variation. Unlike the court dances of earlier centuries, which were often followed to the letter from royal court to royal court, country dance has been the whims and wishes of the individual dancers in each area, without regard to what anyone in another region was doing.

Probably the earliest dances to be done in this country were the contra dances of New England. These dances were democratic in form—with everyone pretty much equal on the dance floor—and often were styled around American Revolutionary themes and paeans to early American heroes. These group or round dances thus served not only to unite all citizens under a single cause, but also to provide the rest of the world with a symbol of America's fight for independence. Many of the die-hard Puritans of the era, of course, denounced such dancing as sacrilegious and evil. Consequently, some people simply did *not* dance. However, other religious leaders—often representing the same church—interpreted scripture quite differently, advocating participation in dance as a healthy and innocent celebration of wholesome urges. The theory that dance was a natural and beneficial form of recreation was supported by the fact that it survived, and today New Englanders still participate in and preserve their dance traditions.

Another early dance form, clogging, was first adopted in black and white southern rural areas. Focusing on routines that included loud taps on the floor made by the dancers' feet, this style was often considered vulgar by the sophisticated urbanites of the era. It did, however, spread to other rural areas in North America, and now can be seen in such diverse locales as French Canada, Nova Scotia, and New England.

In the early American west, dance styles tended to be even more diverse, with the huge influx of immigrants from all corners of the western world contributing a step here and a hop there. Along with the 19th-century flow of immigrants from Great Britain came the Scottish and Irish jigs. In addition, families that had resided in America for

Even today, his saddle is often the cowboy's most prized possession.
(Courtesy of the El Paso Convention and Visitors Bureau)

Cowboys today might not be as isolated as they once were, but the outdoor life is just as rugged.
(Courtesy of the El Paso Convention and Visitors Bureau)

some time and decided to head for western frontiers brought with them dances such as reels, like the Virginia reel, and cotillions. Forerunners of the square dances, the cotillions consisted of spontaneously directed moves called by a fiddler. Like other dance styles throughout history, the cotillions were often considered less than genteel—even scandalous—by those in budding metropolitan areas who were used to following more rigid rules for behavior than were the rugged pioneers of the west.

Whether they danced jigs, reels, or cotillions, these early western dancers mirrored their life-styles in these dances. Holding a dance in a barn or other large meeting area, often outdoors, provided an opportunity for distant neighbors to get together and socialize. They also provided an occasion to look forward to with pleasure for the rough-and-tumble cowboys who were often isolated on the range for months at a time. For all concerned, they offered a healthy and fun way to let off steam, to celebrate a coming spring after a brutal winter, to forget about the rigors of frontier life.

This also was true of the styles adopted in the dances themselves. A good fiddler was one who could play loudly, clearly, and for hours on end, and who could play fast-tempo tunes such that all those within earshot—from toddler to grandmother—just had to tap their feet. These whirling dances often left the dancers breathless and flushed. A lot of foot-stomping, hooting, and drinking was likely to take place, and even if a brawl or two occurred from time to time, everyone at the cotillion was likely to know that the goal of most participants was nothing but good clean fun.

As the west grew in population and immigrants continued to pour into the country, other European dances crept into the western barn dances and dance halls. Soon, country dancers had adapted polkas and waltzes to their own styles, and they even began to create their own forms of dance. One type, which appeared during the late 19th century, was known as "swinging." Probably one of the most exhilarating dance forms found anywhere, it involved couples who danced with their hands on each other's waists or shoulders and twirled around the floor at a breakneck pace. This, too, was frowned upon by etiquette experts, but that didn't stop the "swingers" of the old west.

As time moved on, particular regions eventually chose their own favorites and developed their own renditions of all the dances they had gathered from the eastern U.S. and the countries of Europe. The wide-open nature of the west continued to urge ranchers and townspeople alike to hold social get-togethers. The rowdy nature of the dances also was retained, as westerners of the 19th and early 20th centuries continued to lead rough, even spartan, lives that called for the relief of music and dancing and for socializing with members of the opposite sex.

As urban centers sprouted up across the west, country dance began to take a back seat to the more sophisticated ballroom dances of the 1920s, '30s, and '40s. Often, the barn-type dance was revived only as a commemorative occasion in which the participants once again donned the "costumes" of their forefathers. However, it is important to note that the dance form and its trappings *were* retained, perhaps out of no other motivation than a regional pride in the ways of the pioneers who helped to build their country.

Retention of the traditional dances of the old west was encouraged during the

Cowboy duds haven't changed much since the old days. Western shirts in checks and plaids of bright colors are matched with a variety of hats in every material and style.
(Courtesy of the El Paso Convention and Visitors Bureau)

Like the mechanical bull at Gilley's Club, this rope-and-barrel rig helps train rodeo riders.
(Courtesy of the El Paso Convention and Visitors Bureau)

mid-20th century by such notable figures as Lloyd ("Pappy") Shaw and his wife Dorothy Shaw, who formed the Cheyenne Mountain Dancers of the 1940s. The Shaws and their company helped renew interest in square dancing. They wrote books on the subject, published a magazine, and even helped to popularize barn dances again. To this day, proponents of square dancing and similar dance forms offer clubs, lessons, and publications on this form of recreation. However, it is unlikely that square dancing will ever take a place in everyone's weekly activities to the extent that disco dancing, for example, has in today's urban and suburban communities. Without playing to the modern citizen, no traditional form of dance is likely to become a solid part of our culture. And this is what cowboy dancing is all about.

From tradition and an earlier age, country dancing of the 1980s takes its basic dance styles and names, and the image and values of the American cowboy. From the present, the country dance world has gleaned modern country music, dance halls in the spirit of 20th-century bars or clubs with dance floors, and, of course, the young fans looking for a good time that may not end with the last call from the bar.

This unusual combination of old and new conspires to bring America a great way to spend Saturday night—especially for those who are disenchanted with rock concerts and discotheques. It could be said that the folks who hit Gilley's every Saturday night without fail are looking for the same thing as those who head for Studio 54—an escape into fantasy. But the type of fantasy world provided by the western dance hall is a totally different thing than that provided by a discotheque. Where disco fans seek glamor and spotlights as refuge from humdrum urban life, western dancers tend to

In the old days, many city slickers considered the American cowboy just about as wild and woolly as the bulls they roped.

seek the simplicity and independence of the cowboy life. The disco fan and the country fan do tend to have one thing in common, of course: Neither bears any real resemblance to the type of character he or she is emulating at their respective hangouts. The flashiest disco dancer is likely to be an accountant during the day, and the most impressive of urban cowboys are likely to be just that—average citizens who work at less-than-inspiring, physically tiring jobs in the industrial centers of the country.

In order to understand the appeal of the country dance world, let's examine the American cowboy and his life style.

The Legend of the American Cowboy

From the time we are young children through our autumn years—and from the 19th century through the modern space age—we have always been fascinated by the life led by the great American cowboy. The cowboy symbolized courage and guts—the ultimate in manliness—and served as a hero figure for youngsters and oldsters alike who knew nothing of the hardships involved but could think of nothing more exciting than riding the range with the best of them.

The cowboy had to have guts and nerve just to ride his horse, since physical injury of some sort was almost guaranteed to be part of his job. He had to be skillful in performing his duties, since his life—isolated as he was—might depend on it. And he had to have the toughness and fortitude to live almost all alone.

The cowboy also lived by very strict moral and other codes. Besides his love for his horse and saddle, the cowboy had great respect for women. He saw women as lofty creatures and often put them on a pedestal. One legendary cowboy was heard to say to a woman who swore in public, "For God's sake, woman, why can't you let us look up to you?" And another was wont to say that the only two things a cowboy feared were being set afoot and a decent woman.

Cowboys were the epitome of the strong silent type of man. The fact that they encountered few other people on the range led them to adopt a combination of cheerfulness and reserve toward strangers. It wasn't considered fitting to be inhospit-able to a stranger, but no cowboy would be foolish enough to immediately trust just anyone who came down the pike. Their isolation also made cowboys men of few words who might not know the right thing to say at all times in polite society, but who would come up with down-to-earth poetry in describing the things with which they were most familiar. One cowboy's simple eloquence was evidenced in this obser-vation about the Grand Canyon: "God dug that there hole in anger, and painted it in joy."

Probably the most interesting parallel between the old-time cowboy and today's urban cowboy is their independence. Cowboys past and present were self-reliant, stood up for their rights and their beliefs, and because of the nature of their job, often took orders from no one from day to day. However, this independence in no way indicated an independence of wealth or that associated with a high social standing. As opposed to the rancher who was his boss, the cowboy was almost always broke,

An urban cowboy pauses during a game of pool at one of the forty tables that dot the floor at Gilley's Club.

and his independence stretched only to his isolation on the range and, most importantly, to the fact that he was doing what he wanted to do; he had chosen to be a cowboy, despite the hardships involved. This is true of the cowboys at places like Gilley's as well. They are not free in that they still must hold some type of nine-to-five job, but in most cases in locations like Texas, those jobs often involve difficult and dangerous work. In other words, the urban cowboy also could be called the industrial cowboy.

The cowboys and cowgirls of today's dance halls stick to the traditional cowboy values, and even wear some of the traditional cowboy attire. They, like their earlier counterparts, head for places like Gilley's to let off steam and to leave their rough daily lives behind. They go to hustle those of the opposite sex, to prove their mettle on the dance floor, at the punching bag, and on the mechanical bull. They guzzle Lone Star beer and swagger around the clubs in their cowboy boots. And the result is that Texas in all its cowboy glory is being transplanted to cities as diverse as New York, Boston, Chicago, Phoenix, and others. There's no telling where it will all end.

The "professor" of mechanical bull riding.

The crowd at the American Library Association gala held at Gilley's in Dallas wore a full spectrum of western-type outfits. (Courtesy of Arthur Plotnik)

CHAPTER 3

DANCE HALLS AND HONKY TONKS

Country and western clubs of all descriptions have always been around, but recently in America they have been relegated to small, single-minded southern and western towns where the times don't change all that fast and country is the only real music in the world. This is not to say that a good cowboy hideout or two cannot be found in just about every major city—east or west, north or south. But these country oases, erected for those who hanker for a good country sound no matter where they are, often are hard to find. Unless they bill well-known c&w stars, they are not likely to advertise widely, and in cities dominated by disco and rock they remain in the night-life background.

In most American cities, it may be even more difficult to locate a country club that features kicker dancing, or dancing of any kind for that matter. While a lot of foot stomping and hand clapping is certainly inherent in a country music club, few clubs feature a really functional dance floor. Of course, you can probably find a local square dance or barn dance club in your vicinity, or you can check out scattered honky tonks and country-oriented road houses if you live in or near a rural area. But the true country dance hall is just beginning to spread across the nation.

As we move into the 1980s, many signs indicate that the country dance hall or club may prove to be one of the most enduring sources of recreation of the century. Several factors come into play in this evolution toward simple western pleasure. First of all, country music is more popular today than ever before, with well-known rock, pop, and folk musicians bringing down-home music to the urban masses through radio, TV, film, and recordings. Rock fans of old are picking up on bluegrass and rockabilly like never before, disco fans are learning the allure of the country beat, folks of all ages hum to simple ballads, and just about everyone loves the homey country lyrics.

This rousing rendition of the Bunny Hop is not for the weary.

I'm proud to be a KIKKer!

In keeping with this trend, as pop artists pick up the style that says country, country musicians who originally catered to purist listeners now are writing their songs and keying their arrangements to the tastes of the broader pop audience. From the visit of Willie Nelson to the White House to the rising ratings achieved by country music programs on network television, the nation is being treated to a fascinating new introduction to the world of country music. Even the famous music publication *Rolling Stone* recently featured an article on the new image for country music and its stars, "Crossing Over: A Two-Way Street—Country Music Sees the Promi$ed Land."

Another factor that has contributed greatly to the rise of the country dance hall is America's renewed interest in dance in general. Disco, ironically, has done its part merely by spreading the dance craze across the world. People of all ages have now returned to the dance floor, encouraged by physical fitness advocates who endorse dancing as a fun way to get your daily exercise. The nation's new fascination with the dance world has encouraged participants to seek out new forms of their favorite recreational activity.

The results? One interesting symptom of this fast-growing trend comes to us from Texas, as do a lot of the aspects of the country dance world. This is daytime dancing, which has been common in Texas for at least twenty-five years and has now spread from the Lone Star State to such far horizons as Los Angeles and Minneapolis. Housewives and lunching officeworkers flock at noon to places like Dallas's Palms Danceland. Such spots have been tagged "pressure cookers" and "microwave clubs" in reference to the fact that participating housewives tend to rush home straight from the dance floor to slap together a quick supper for their families.

The pro-western trend, furthered to a great extent by fashion designers who have begun introducing whole lines of western garb for men and women, has appeared in places as unlikely as a recent American Library Association party, at which everyone came in western style. Country has even infiltrated the most dedicated discotheques. In some cases, certain evenings are designated country nights, and in others a separate country room has been added to a club. An example of the latter is the Chicago-area Barn of Barrington, which already featured a popular restaurant and disco before it added a country dance room complete with lessons available to patrons.

Clubs devoted solely to country also are beginning to sprout in the large cities of the U.S. Some of them may not be considered the real thing by those who hail from Houston, but their efforts are sincere and their patrons satisfied for the most part. It all started, and is still concentrated of course, in Texas. Among other popular spots in that state is the Longhorn Ballroom in Dallas. Arizona has its share of country clubs, particularly in the cities of Phoenix and Tucson. Los Angeles has picked up the trend, as would be expected. And country clubs can now be found in large eastern cities such as New York, which boasts the Lone Star Cafe in Manhattan.

GILLEY'S CLUB

If you really want to be initiated properly, however, there's no better place to begin your country education than at Gilley's Club, in Pasadena, Texas, near the southeastern border of Houston. Gilley's is generally agreed to be the Number One cowboy dance hall—the honky tonk to end all honky tonks. Gilley's was born inauspiciously as Shelly's, an inconspicuous bar located at 4500 Spencer Highway that held about 500 people, and owned by one Sherwood Cryer. As the unassuming dance hall began to draw more and more industrial cowboys and cowgirls, Cryer blithely tacked on more and more square-footage to create a rambling, warehouse-type bar that currently holds 4,500 patrons when a hot musician fills the place to its limits.

With the aid of country music star Mickey Gilley (see chapter 4 for more on Gilley), Cryer has created one of the most awesome sights a newcomer could ever hope to see. Chic and elegance have no place at Gilley's, which is plastered with ceiling tiles printed with the famous Gilley's script logo, and whose walls are plastered with banners welcoming rodeo fans, signs proclaiming upcoming one-night stands of such country greats as Waylon Jennings and George Jones, and entrance and exit doors that inform all that "Through these doors pass the greatest entertainers and

Mickey Gilley International Fan Club

4500 SPENCER HIGHWAY - PASADENA, TEXAS 77504

New Member ________

Renewal Member ________

NAME ________________________________

ADDRESS ________________________________

CITY ____________ STATE ____________ ZIP CODE ____________

BIRTHDAY ____________ CLUB RECOMMENDED BY: ____________

MEMBERSHIP DUES: $5.00 U.S. and CANADA
$10.00 Overseas

MEMBERSHIP PRIVILEGES: Membership card, 8 x 10 autographed photo of MICKEY, fan club badge and 4 Newsletters per year (issued in MARCH, JUNE, SEPTEMBER, and DECEMBER).

Member INTERNATIONAL FAN CLUB ORGANIZATION

Gilley's humble decorating scheme goes unnoticed when one of the standard country greats gets up on the music stage.

customers in the world." The walls are covered with rough-hewn wood and are sparked by neon signs for Lone Star, Miller, and other beer brands; the floors are scuffed and sans underlighting; the pool tables, chairs and tables have all taken a beating; and the parking lot overflows with battered pickup trucks.

If owner and operator Cryer thought the place couldn't get much more popular than when the locals showed up in droves—somehow managing to fill the entire place almost nightly—then he must have been flabbergasted at the nationwide attention the place has received in recent months. Articles on Gilley's Club and Mickey Gilley himself have appeared in magazines like *Esquire* and *US,* and in newspapers like the *Washington Post* and the *Houston Post.* Gilley has been a guest on shows such as the Dinah Shore Show and the Merv Griffin Show, and Tom Brokaw filmed action and interviews at the club for NBC-TV's Today Show. To top it all off, the bittersweet story of a Gilley's regular, as written in *Esquire,* has been adapted for an upcoming film, *Urban Cowboy,* starring none other than John Travolta in the leading male role.

What is it that forms the mystique that attracts country dancers of all ages,

Employees sporting all types of Gilley's memorabilia draw Lone Star beer and keep the popcorn machines running.

The bouncer at Gilley's lays his bulk into the mechanical punching bag.

Hollywood celebrities as well as oil-refinery workers, and easterners and westerners to a place like Gilley's? If nothing else, the club is an experience. The magazine articles, features, news coverage, stars of radio, TV, and movies, and just plain folk are all a part of that special feeling that is Gilley's. The man in the coveralls who walks around unobtrusively is Sherwood Cryer himself. It is he who owns the 100-plus amusement devices that line the walls, and the nearly forty pool tables that dot the floor. It is he who drives a pickup truck with a Gilley's bumpersticker when he could well afford a Rolls Royce and a chauffeur. This quiet man who loves the club so much seems to be a great part of the club's mystique.

The same people show up at Gilley's night after night to dance to the house band, the Bayou City Beats, and to ride the mechanical bull that was designed to train rodeo riders. They come to demonstrate their prowess at the coin-operated punching bag that emits a wail from a siren when someone really unleashes a strong right. They come to hustle the girls and to play a little pool. Wearing Gilley's t-shirts and belt buckles and their own cowboy boots and hats, they come to the club in almost a

ritualistic exercise of latter-day manhood. It is here that men are men and girls are girls. As we discussed in chapter 2, the urban or industrial cowboys and their cowgirls come to Gilley's to let off a little steam and to fulfill a fantasy of a simpler era that helps them return to their dreary and often physically dangerous jobs in the refineries and petrochemical plants that surround Houston. And the atmosphere offered by Gilley's seems to suit a lot of easterners, too—especially those who find no satisfaction from the fantasy world offered at their local discotheque. Gilley's attracts drinkers, dancers, and fighters of all ages, couples and singles alike. It provides a huge arena for getting acquainted with members of the opposite sex, or a great place to show your stuff after getting kicked around by the "system" all day long.

Besides dancing and chasing women (or men), Gilley's offers a slew of other

Gilley's huge dance floor fills with kickers of all ages for one of the popular line dances.

activities for the restless. You can drink at any one of four bars, sit at a table and watch the crowd, or simply amble around the huge club, mingling for hours without feeling like you've seen it all. If you don't want to try your hand at the punching bag or the pool tables, you can join the crowd on the dance floor, hang around and listen to DJs from local radio stations that broadcast live from Gilley's on weekends, or have your fill of popcorn or barbecue from the ever-open kitchen.

The huge mechanical bull always draws a large audience, as well as numerous rodeo challengers. Operated by an expert, the bull bucks around so hard that some say it's harder to ride than the real thing. In fact, you have to sign a waiver stating that you're riding it at your own risk and you won't hold the club responsible in case of injury, which is not all that uncommon. The bull offers the cowboys a chance to prove

Originally designed to train rodeo riders, this mechanical bull is said to be tougher to ride than the real thing, but that doesn't stop most of Gilley's regulars from taking their turn on its back.

Forewarned is forearmed!

their manhood, and in the spirit of the late 20th century, the women have begun to challenge and beat the men at their own game. On any given night, you're bound to see a rough-and-ready cowgirl bouncing nonchalantly up and down on the bull's back and taunting surrounding cowboys for being shown up by a girl. Both the bull and the punching bag were installed by owner Cryer in an effort to channel the patrons' aggressive instincts away from brawls and into a less destructive pastime. Cryer insists there have been fewer fights since he added these attractions, but you still might see a rumble or two of small proportions at the club. This is not the sort of place where irritated patrons bother asking their opponents to step outside.

Among the crazier events held at Gilley's are the few weddings that have been held there, officiated by old-fashioned Judge West of Pasadena. And this year, Gilley's held a Dolly Parton look-alike contest that attracted national attention.

Those who end up being regulars at Gilley's practically make the place their whole leisure-time world. Besides showing up every night and carefully choosing and taking care of the exactly correct cowboy outfit for their visits, these fans are likely to sport Gilley's belt buckles, baseball caps, and t-shirts. They'll tell time by Gilley's calendars, and proudly point to the Gilley's bumperstickers on their pickups. (It is said that if you park your vehicle at Gilley's and fail to put your visors down, you'll be presented with a bumpersticker, whether you wanted one or not.) If you hang out at Gilley's at all regularly, you're bound to leave the place with a nickname of your own—nobody at Gilley's goes by his given name for long. Gilley's now produces a glossy newsletter with information on the latest doings at the club and its adjacent recording studio. And if you really want to do it up right, you can now buy a six-pack of Gilley's beer.

So regular and so dedicated was one customer of Gilley's, Eddie (Dew) Westbrook, that an *Esquire* article about him and his experiences at the club will soon foster a movie. With John Travolta of *Saturday Night Fever* fame playing the part of Dew in *Urban Cowboy,* America will be treated to country dance and flash as authentic as the old west itself. Dew Westbrook came to dance and hustle girls and to ride the mechanical bull at Gilley's. Arguments over the bull and its inherent danger were the beginning of the end for the marriage of Dew and his Gilley's-met girlfriend, Betty, and the movie tells the whole heart-wrenching story of how boy met girl, boy married girl, boy divorced girl and went with another—all at Gilley's and all smacking of the "he done me wrong" flavor of a country music ballad.

While no one knows how Travolta will fare against the bull in *Urban Cowboy,* he is said to have picked up the country dance style with the best of them. Taught and coached by Gilley's employee Peggy Wright, who appears in the instructional photos in chapter 6, Travolta engages in a dance contest during the movie against Gator who also appears in our photos.

For more information on the music these high-steppers trot out on the floor for, turn the page to chapter 4.

Just one of the many country musicians to hit Hollywood, Jerry Reed recently appeared in the movie "Smokey and the Bandit," starring Burt Reynolds.
(Courtesy of RCA Records)

PICKERS AND WAILERS—COUNTRY MUSICIANS

These days, when someone mentions country music, you cannot be sure exactly what type of music is meant. Just twenty-five years ago, country was likely to mean country and western music and to be enjoyed mainly by those who lived in rural areas and listened to no other music forms. Today, however, when the term "country music" is used, it could indicate not only country and western, but bluegrass, rockabilly, gospel, folk ballads, southern country rock, and many other subcategories. To the purist, of course, an indescribable something makes a country song country and nothing else. But for those newcomers to the world of country tunes, anything that features a lively fiddle, a female vocalist with a twangy vibrato, or sentimental lyrics chock full of down-home poetry is country music.

Like country or cowboy dancing, the differences between various types of country music often are regional. Bluegrass, obviously, comes from good ol' bluegrass country; rockabilly stems mainly from the southern mountains; and folk tunes from various eras have been popular with folks in the most sophisticated metropolises of America. From California come popular bands like "Asleep at the Wheel," which feature the newly booming western swing sound. And from eastern Texas dance halls like Gilley's comes that old honky tonk kicker style. In keeping with the times, you might even hear some dyed-in-the-wool rock or blues bands pouring forth their rendition of country music over a jukebox or radio that also features pure country. The Allman Brothers, the Rolling Stones, and female singers like Linda Ronstadt and Bonnie Rait have all produced individual songs that are popular among country lovers.

Experts on the subject of current musical trends would call this just one sign of the country-pop crossover that has contributed in large measure to the recent country music and dance boom. On the surface, there seems to be no particular reason why an unprecedented country boom should take place now, at the beginning of the '80s.

Suddenly, the country music industry, which has been characterized in the past by a laid-back, no-hustle attitude toward success, seems to have exploded into a fury of star-making publicity and national attention. Why now are country music artists often landing at the top of pop music charts? Why are some of the world's most saleable pop musicians now doing their own arrangements of songs written by Hank Williams and his contemporary followers? Why, for heaven's sake, are country acts replacing the chorus lines in Vegas?

Recording industry insiders feel that this move could possibly be traced to the Big Buck. They believe that country artists are leaning toward more widely appealing pop arrangements these days because of simple dollars and cents. As late as the 1970s, for example, a country star whose tune hit Number One on the charts could realistically hope for no more than 300,000 sales. *Any* Number One pop hit, on the other hand, could sell millions of copies. In addition, the attraction of the simpler life—as manifested in country music and dance—has proved strong enough to draw thousands and thousands of newcomers to the country scene. And what the public wants, the public gets: More and more television air time is devoted to country programs; pop and other artists are experimenting, and succeeding, with country styles and songs; and the fashion industry is going along with the trend quite happily, turning out newer (and often more expensive) versions of western and even American Indian styles. What all of this adds up to is a hugely profitable new business with great promise for going nowhere but up.

Even the associations and organizations that serve the country music world have been affected by the sudden onslaught of westernmania. As is the case when any change begins to rear its head, there are those who prefer to maintain the status quo. During the mid-1970s, after pop star Olivia Newton-John walked away with some annual awards given by the Nashville-based Country Music Association, some of the country purists got together to form an organization called the Association of Country Entertainers. Its purpose was to protect the purity of country music, or, bluntly, to prevent pop stars like Newton-John from supplanting "real" country stars in the limelight and elsewhere. Strangely enough, the Association not only proved to be short-lived, but some of its strongest proponents—Dolly Parton among them—ended up furthering the crossover between pop and country by aiming their recordings at the pop audience.

Another sign of the current meshing of pop and country styles was in the 1979 Country Music Association annual awards. The Charlie Daniels Band—albeit country-like but known mainly as a rock band—grabbed three of the highest awards available.

Nashville, that self-contained capital of country music, has also been infiltrated by other styles of music. According to *Rolling Stone,* about 37,000 recording sessions were held in that city's studios during a single year in the late '70s, and two-thirds of those sessions involved noncountry styles of music. Predictably, more and more true country artists are recording their albums in cities and towns nowhere near Tennessee. You'll hear the twangs of a country picker emanating from the walls of studios in such far-reaching locations as New York, Toronto, and San Francisco. And as a significant example, current stars like Mickey Gilley are leaving the Nashville nest and

The booming country scene has been helped along by such widely popular stars as Dolly Parton.
(Courtesy of RCA Records)

making a success with studios of their own. Gilley's studio is adjacent to Gilley's Club in Pasadena, Texas, and the first album Gilley recorded there was lauded as his best ever by critics.

Over the last decade, some musicians have disappeared from pop or rock charts, only to reappear on the country scene, and then repeat the whole cycle over and over again. Emmylou Harris, for instance, is an example of the enigmatic artists who do not fall into one particular category but are considered basically country by many listeners and musicians. Emmylou has played with such greats as Gram Parsons and sung backup vocals with rock and country stars, but although she's a pretty constant favorite with country fans, she has not been all that successful in the world of pop music.

Other musicians have turned to country for a comeback or revival of their waning stardom. Bob Dylan, for instance, has thrown his old-time fans for a loop with his recently released album *Slow Train Coming,* which has been labeled as white gospel in style. Musicians such as Tanya Tucker, Kenny Rogers, and others have almost always lived in both the country and the pop worlds. Interestingly, new-wave artist Elvis Costello has even jumped into the act. Recently Costello made the pilgrimage to Nashville in order to record a duet with veteran George Jones, who is said to be one of his longtime idols.

To top it all off, country music stars are getting into the movie business as well. Nashville comes to Hollywood in the next year or so with appearances by Mickey Gilley and others in the film *Urban Cowboy,* with the upcoming film based on Kenny Rogers's album *The Gambler,* and with guest appearances in several movies by Jerry Reed.

GILLEY'S MUSIC

If there's one thing at Gilley's that an outsider would immediately recognize as deserving of the crowds it draws, it is the music at Gilley's. If you don't believe it could be that good, all you have to do is take one look at the awesome sight of, say, 3,000 people dancing, stomping their feet, or singing along with popular lyrics. It is probably appropriate that the world's largest nightclub (according to Guiness) should be owned by a couple of men with such diverse talents as Sherwood Cryer and Mickey Gilley. (See chapter 3 for more details on Cryer.) Mickey Gilley spent nearly twenty years working, promoting, singing, and playing piano in an effort to come up with a hit. Finally, he scored the big one by sweeping the awards at the 12th annual Academy of Country Music awards. The west-coast-based organization presented him with no fewer than six awards: Entertainer of the Year, Male Singer of the Year, Country Song of the Year for "Don't the Girls Get Prettier at Closing Time," Single Record of the Year for "Bring It on Home to Me," Album of the Year for "Gilley's Smokin'," and Best Touring Band for his own Red Rose Express.

Mickey Gilley grew up as one of the "three piano pickers from Ferriday (Louisiana)" along with cousins Jerry Lee Lewis and Jimmy Swaggart. While Lewis proceeded to become a well-known country star, the reticent Gilley struggled along in

Co-owner of Gilley's Club in Pasadena, Texas, Mickey Gilley is a veteran star of the c&w music world.
(Courtesy of Epic Records)

the background. Ironically, Gilley spent ten out of twenty hard years (1960 to 1970) at the Nesadel, a club down the highway from the current Gilley's, which Gilley's regulars scorn (one of them proclaiming that he wouldn't go near the Nesadel without at least ten of his fellow cowboys along). Gilley was about forty years old when he finally hit the big time, but apparently it was worth the wait. Between 1976 and 1978, at least ten of Gilley's tunes hit the Top 10, and now he's said to be heading for the stages of Las Vegas, among other things. Gilley, too, has been accused of crossing over into the pop world, especially with his super-popular album *Songs We Made Love To,* but he swears that if any hint of rock or pop that appears in his newer releases offends his country fans, he'll banish it entirely from his repertoire. Like most other country/pop/rock stars, his first love and allegiance is always to country.

The titles and lyrics of Gilley's most popular songs, like those of other artists heard at the club, reflect the simple and sometimes sentimental appeal of country themes. They also demonstrate the wry humor concerning the urban cowboy's life style and the rowdy nose-thumbing attitude toward humdrum jobs and the modern world in general. Some of Gilley's most famous tunes include "The Power of Positive Drinking," "Honky Tonk Wine," "A Room Full of Roses," and "Just Long Enough to Say Goodbye." Another predictably popular song at Gilley's is "Take This Job and Shove It."

Even Gilley's studio is not limited to the recording of pure country tunes. Diverse musicians such as Archie Bell and the Drells and Arnett Cobb have recorded alongside Mickey and his compatriots, and one of Mickey's fondest dreams is said to be recording several "Live at Gilley's Club" albums that would feature major country artists from across the nation.

The music offered on a given evening at Gilley's Club is, of course, a lot more than Mickey Gilley himself tickling the ivories. In fact, Mickey's appearances at the club are pretty rare these days, as he divides his limited time among recording sessions, road tours, and appearances on such TV talk shows as the Dinah Shore Show and the Merv Griffin Show.

A wide variety of country greats are played over the jukebox at Gilley's until around 9:15 each evening, when the live music takes over. At that time, the Bayou City Beats, the house band, hit the stage for a grueling five-hour set with short breaks. Featuring Norman Carlson on the sax and Robert ("The Little Fiddler") Herridge, the Beats keep Gilley's rocking until the wee hours. The band also features star vocalists Johnny Lee, Toni Jolene, and Kenny Fulton, and some truly great Nashville singers who drift in for one-nighters. Among those that have appeared at Gilley's in the past are Waylon Jennings, Johnny Bush, George Jones, Fats Domino, Johnny Russell, Billy "Crash" Craddock, Chubby Wise, Cal Smith, and Willie Nelson. When Willie appeared at Gilley's, a full 4,500 fans packed themselves into Gilley's for the experience. Other stars tend to drop in unannounced and often unnoticed. For instance, Tanya Tucker once sat at a corner table, just blending in with the other patrons, and going unnoticed by the crowd until she joined the Bayou City Beats onstage for a rousing rendition of "Help Me Make It Through the Night."

One of the biggest of such surprises was the appearance one afternoon, and later that evening, of John Travolta as he cased the joint in preparation for playing the

Jerry Lee Lewis is probably the most famous of the "three piano pickers from Ferriday" that also included cousins Mickey Gilley and Jimmy Swaggart. (Courtesy of Elektra Records)

role of a Gilley's regular in the film *Urban Cowboy.* If Gilley's was not on the map before the whole movie scene hit Pasadena, then afterward it surely was known by nation-wide fans. Such well-known bands as the Eagles and singers Linda Ronstadt, Jimmy Buffett, Waylon Jennings, and, of course, Mickey, were possible musical stars of the movie as well.

The 1980 Winter Olympic Games go western with these Levi Strauss overalls for women and vest-and-jean outfits for men. All garments shown are made by Levi Strauss, and the denim garments, embossed with the Olympic rings symbol, are part of the U.S. athletes' casual wardrobe for leisure time during the games.

CHAPTER 5

KICKER FASHIONS AND COWBOY DUDS

Nowhere is America's new interest in the old west more evident than in the fashions in vogue today. From red bandanas to cowboy boots with pointed toes, the western look has faded in and out of fashion over the years, but it is only recently that everyone in the clothing industry—from haute-couture designers to the huge blue jean manufacturers—has put it all together to come up with the total cowboy image.

The widespread availability of western attire actually may have furthered the cowboy movement in this country and elsewhere, but at the very least it can be interpreted as a sign of the fad's grand success and growth. It is common for the movers and shapers in the huge international fashion industry to pick up on the latest sociological trends, and the fascination with things western has been no exception. Shops featuring western clothing have been appearing alongside boutiques that star disco clothes, and even department stores have been getting into the act with the addition of new western departments. Even some of the long-lived mail-order houses that have always featured western-flavor outdoorwear are enjoying increased sales.

Literally all types of people of every age are sporting western garb for nearly every occasion. Smart fashion leaders hardly needed to be convinced of the appeal that westernwear would have for today's urban dwellers as well as their rural counterparts. Rural people of all ages and young people from all types of communities have, of course, been wearing blue jeans and leather boots for informal occasions for years. However, now it is likely that you will see the most fashion-conscious of city sophisticates swaggering around a chic cocktail party in their ornately tooled leather outfits and highly polished boots—and receiving just as many compliments on their attire as those dressed in the lushest of silks and satins.

One of the greatest attractions of western attire for the general public is its comfort. The casual styles and somewhat loose fit of these clothes suit the active life

Youngsters emulate their favorite heroes and heroines in Levi's® Youthwear jeans with matching vests and colorful plaid western shirts.

styles followed by most modern Americans. And in a day of plastic everything, cost-conscious buyers often seek out the durable natural fabrics—leather, cotton and wool, for example—that most western garments feature. This is not to say, of course, that western clothing is always inexpensive. On the contrary, these sturdy leathers and comfortable cloths tend to be more expensive than manmade materials, but the buyer of natural materials often realizes that he or she is getting more for the money spent.

CLASSIC COWBOY DUDS

While today's western outfits do reflect the basic components of the original cowboy's

Girls can take on the western look with Levi's® belted holster skirt paired with an all-cotton shirt in plain flannel.

ensemble, in detail and in function they bear little resemblance to the clothing worn by the rough riders of the range. The following is a brief summary of the general look adopted by the traditional cowboy of the 19th and early 20th centuries.

There probably is nothing that identified a cowboy as a cowboy so much as his hat. In fact, Hollywood furthered the myth that the color of a cowboy's hat actually indicated his position in society—white hats were worn by the good guys and black hats by the bad guys. In actuality, true cowboys' hats usually were dove gray or light brown, with an occasional black hat appearing on the range. Cowboys wore hats that did, however, signify the part of the west from which they came. Texas and Montana styles were worn, as well as an occasional Mexican sombrero in the southwest.

The ultimate urban cowboy looks to Levi Strauss for a fashionable wool blazer, flannel shirt, and jeans.

Different types of creases were designed and worn by cowboys with differing jobs—bull-riding, cutting-horse riders, and so on. The standard hat featured a seven-inch-high cylindrical crown and often was decorated by a band of woven wire of silver or gold. Silver conchas and rattlesnake skins were sometimes added for color.

The cowboy's hat served many purposes: It shielded his head and face from the sun, and its extra-wide brim was often pulled down to protect the back of his neck from sun and wind. It kept him dry during rain and snow storms and cool during the heat of mid-summer. It also served as a handy bucket.

The bandana, an accessory worn purely for decoration by today's Americans, was also a functional garment for the cowboy. The standard red-and-white or blue-and-white bandana was most often made of cotton, but most cowboys preferred silk. The bandana could be pulled up over the cowboy's face to protect him from dust and wind, and later, when hat brims became narrower, it protected the back of his neck.

The bright paisley and other patterns seen on so-called western shirts had no place in the original cowboy's wardrobe. Their shirts usually were made of wool or cotton with no starch included, and commonly were done up in toned-down checks or stripes. It is interesting that cowboys supposedly never wore red shirts because they believed this color was an aggravation to cattle. Cowboys were not completely immune to vanity even in those days; during the 19th century, when garters were in vogue, cowboys wore them on their shirtsleeves.

The Highland hat from Stetson features a multicolored woven band, a fancy pheasant feather with pom, and the Stetson branding iron pin.

The Stetson Summit offers a 7½-inch bullrider crease crown and a multicolored tapestry woven band.

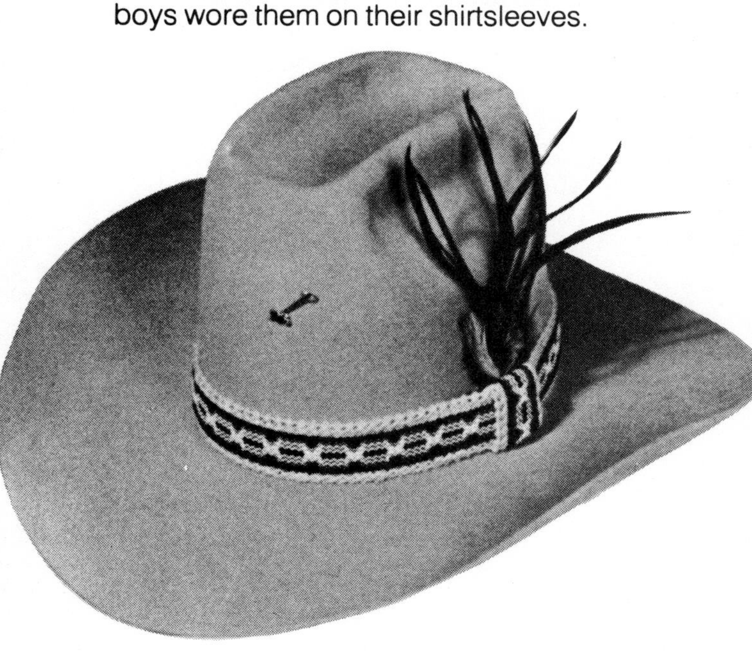

The branding iron pin again appears on Stetson's Escalante, with woven band edged with jute and a large whimsical feather.

El Lobo from Stetson is available for men and women and features a rancher-style crease and pom feather.

Ed Kane's store in Houston features a hat for everyone—every style, every material, every size.

The Beaumont by Stetson has a Canadian crease and bullrider brim, plus a tall pheasant feather with pom.

The Stetson Sundance hat travels from rodeo to office and features a Tite Telescope crease crown and Kettle Curl brim.

The stylish Colter hat by Stetson offers the wearer the flair of the special blown angora finish, along with the standard branding iron pin and colorful feather.

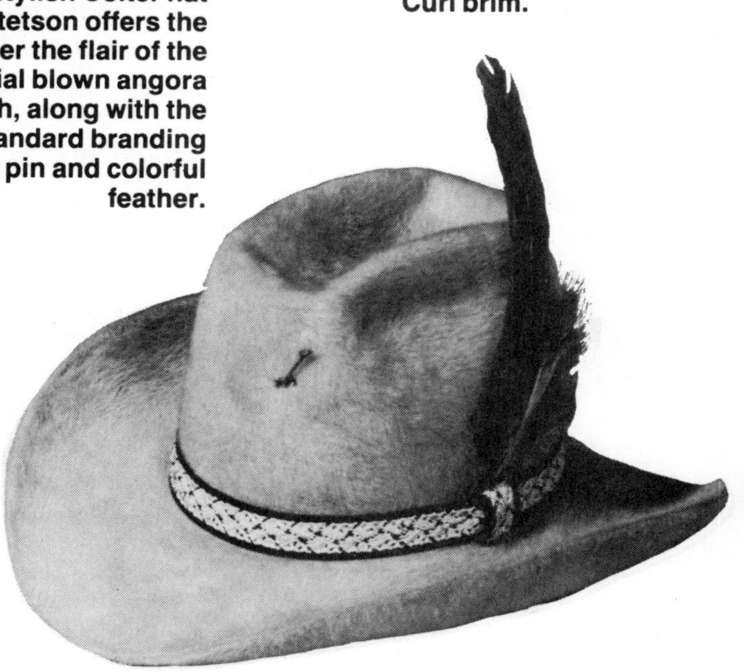

Two of Gilley's Club's regulars show off the attire that helped to make the dance hall famous. Patrons show their loyalty by wearing Gilley's belt buckles to set off their pearl-buttoned shirts and classic dungarees.

Until recent years, the cowboy did not wear blue jeans. Rather, he wore pants in muted colors of wool or in brown or black leather. Cowboys often did without suspenders or belts because they could get in the way and be dangerous to him, but in the southwest cowboys often wore decorative silk sashes of red or green in the Mexican tradition.

Except on the northern ranges, cowboys often wore vests instead of coats. These provided body warmth but left the cowboy's arms free. In the far north, ranchers often provided their cowhands with fur coats and caps.

Chaps are one garment that were purely functional and will rarely be seen on a noncowboy today. The chaps protected the cowboy's legs from scratchy brush that dotted the range and usually were made of white, heavy, dehaired leather or the furry skins of such animals as bears, wolves, dogs, goats, or sheep.

The cowboy boot was as symbolic of his trade as his hat. The original design of the boot was mainly functional, although decorative touches were added for flair in later years. The boots were almost always black, and they featured high uppers and high heels. The high heels, originally intended to prevent the cowboy's feet from slipping out of the stirrups, were thought by some to be just as much an indulgence of

The western shirt is available in suede or deerskin and in women's sizes as well as in men's sizes. Pants are made of elk or cowhide. The prairie blouse and skirt come in soft shades of suede. Both models wear lizard boots to complete the western look. (Courtesy of Preis-Grossman)

Ed Kane's boot selection just possibly might be the largest available under a single roof anywhere.

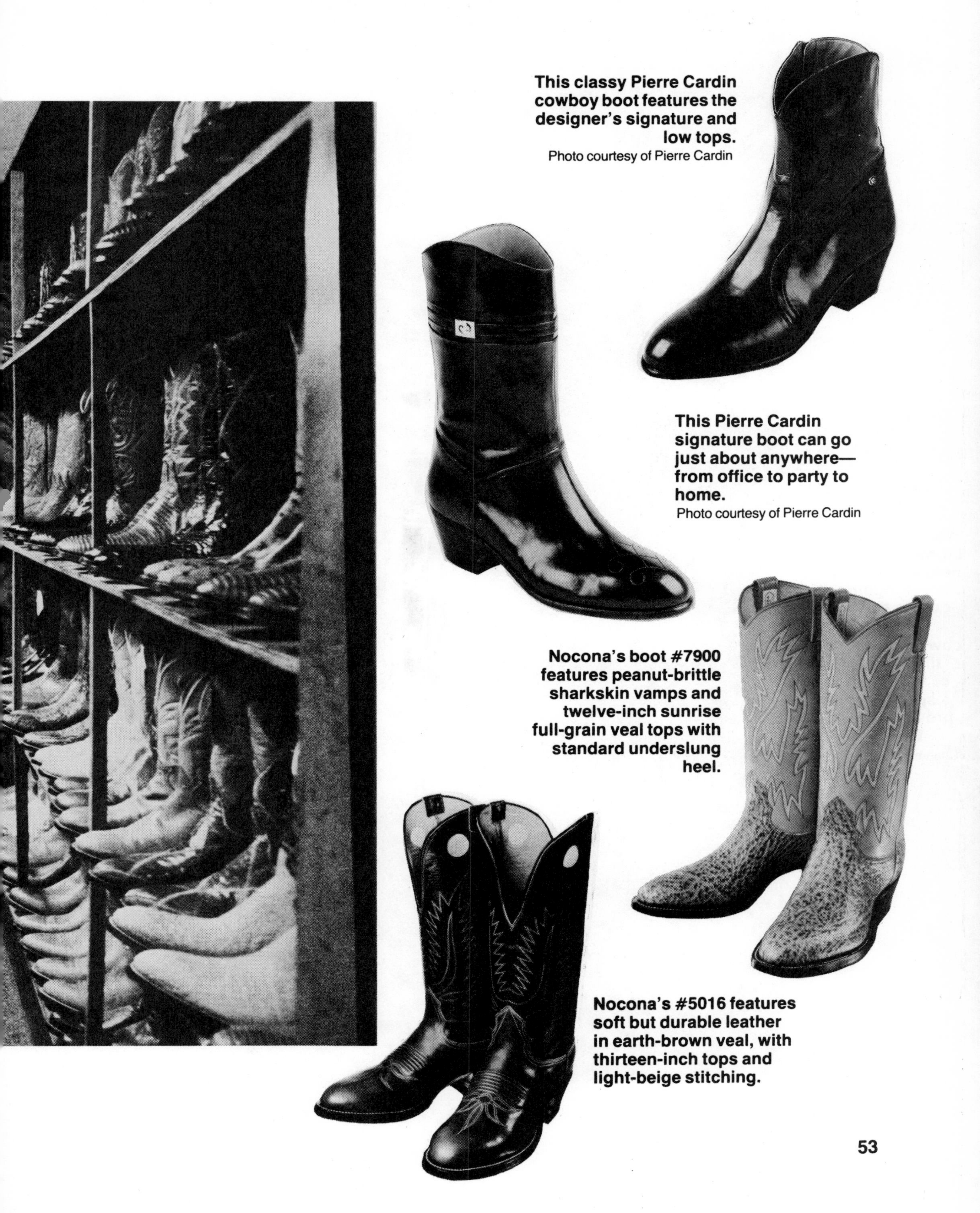

This classy Pierre Cardin cowboy boot features the designer's signature and low tops.
Photo courtesy of Pierre Cardin

This Pierre Cardin signature boot can go just about anywhere—from office to party to home.
Photo courtesy of Pierre Cardin

Nocona's boot #7900 features peanut-brittle sharkskin vamps and twelve-inch sunrise full-grain veal tops with standard underslung heel.

Nocona's #5016 features soft but durable leather in earth-brown veal, with thirteen-inch tops and light-beige stitching.

When the American Library Association held a recent Dallas wingding, the guests showed up in true urban cowboy style. Here, the association's executive director sports garments provided by Cutter Bill's of Dallas.
(Courtesy of Arthur Plotnik)

One of the most attractive features of westernwear for today's urban cowboys is comfort. Wide skirts and well-worn blue jeans make for lively dancing.

vanity. In addition, some cowboy boots began to include decorative tooling and dyes, plus uppers that were higher in the front than in the back—all purely decorative touches. The spurs that could be decorative in themselves were also meant for several uses. They not only helped the cowboy cling to a bucking horse, but they also helped spur on a logy steed.

Gradually, cowboys developed their own set of nonfunctional accessories—some decorative in nature and others worn as symbols of their trade, of which they were unfailingly proud. Intricate horsehair chains were an example. They were used as watch chains or given to lady friends as gifts, and they were considered quite impressive, given the fine detail work handled by the rough hands of the cowboy.

Anne Hollingsworth models clothes from Cutter Bill's Dallas store, completing the look with a leather lariat.
(Courtesy of Arthur Plotnik)

URBAN COWBOY CLOTHING

Today's cowboy wears outfits that are quite similar—especially in function—to those of their forefathers. Of course, some of the materials used have been changed and blue jeans are more common than wool breeches. However, the attire that the noncowboy calls westernwear is quite different.

The urban cowboys and cowgirls spotted at clubs like Gilley's will wear many garments that no true country cowboy would ever wear. For examples, bell-bottom jeans would never be worn by one who spends most of his time on a horse, nor would flat-heeled boots. Short-sleeved shirts would expose the cowboy's arms to wind, rain, snow, and brush. On the decorative side, no true cowboy would have dared to be seen on the range wearing a hat with his name in gold letters on the crown. If he did wear a belt, the traditional cowboy would scorn those that bore gimmick buckles, such as those that bear the name of Gilley's.

Today, the urban cowboy's hat is often as great a source of pride for him as it was for his earlier compatriots. This could be because a hat is expensive, though it's not as much of an income gauge as hats were in the old days. Today's cowboy hats, available mainly from two veteran manufacturers, Stetson and Resistol, sport narrower brims and usually are a white shade called "silver belly." They can cost the cowboy from $40 to $400, whereas the 19th-century cowboy often had to spend two to six months' salary to buy a hat.

Boots have gone the same route. They have been altered for the nonfunctional cowboy, with lower heels and more and more decorative features, and even are available in low uppers. The rhinestone cowboys of the jet set often spend up to a couple of thousand dollars for custom-made boots, and the more ornamental and colorful they are, the better.

Other accessories often worn by the real cowboy will almost never be seen on city cowboys. These include horsehide or buckskin gloves with five-inch gauntlets, tight-fitting leather cuffs, and, naturally, the saddle and its accoutrements.

THE HAUTE COUTURE COWBOY

As is the case when nearly any new cultural trend appears, high-fashion designers from the world over have contributed to the rise of western fashions. Such notables as Pierre Cardin, Ralph Lauren, Adolphe Lafont, Cacharel, and Guy Laroche, among many others, have come out with their own signature lines of everything from bandanas to boots. In addition, high-style boutiques offer one-of-a-kind, custom-made western garments. For both of these types of cowboy clothing, you're likely to pay a pretty penny, but if individuality is your goal, you'll be able to step out in real style with these western additions to your wardrobe.

On the other hand, many manufacturers of boots, blue jeans, and other western-oriented outdoor wear are doing a booming business with their standard items and adding new editions of the basics. For a more affordable cost, you can snap up some decent westernwear made by Levi-Strauss, Lee's, Frye (boots), Stetson and Nocona (hats). You might even check the latest issues of mail-order catalogs from old standby companies such as Schott's and L. L. Bean.

Just about every major city offers at least one western-only boutique or store, and in some cases these marts are so well known that customers travel across the country just to buy their cowboy duds there.

One of the most awesome spots to purchase western clothing is Ed Kane's of Houston. Said to be the largest western store in all of Texas (and that ain't hay), Ed Kane's offers what seem like miles of hats and cowboy boots, in addition to a full regalia of belt buckles, rings, watchboards, and other accessories in the cowboy

Typical of high-end western wear prices, these calfskin jacket-and-pants outfits for men and women are for extravagant buyers. Jackets are trimmed with yokes in snake or ostrich, and the cost of the whole outfit can easily run into three figures.
(Courtesy of Preis-Grossman)

Said to be the largest westernwear store in Texas, Ed Kane's offers everything the urban cowboy could possibly want, on several levels.

style. Another Texas shop, Cutter Bill's of Dallas, is a mecca for high-style westernwear that draws celebrities and other monied types from all corners of the country.

In the midwest, one of the best places to seek out your own version of the cowboy outfit is Laredo in Chicago's Water Tower Place. The most amazing fact about this small but comprehensive store is that the idea for the business came to owner Steve Davis through a visit to a western boutique in Paris, of all cities. Davis was so taken by the fact that the French were grabbing up fashions based on such purely American styles that he figured a Chicago-based western shop was a sure thing. Davis carries only the best in manufacturers and materials, and offers spurs, fringed jackets, and belt buckles, along with the more standard rodeo shirts, boots, and hats. The boots at Laredo are available in every material from plain old leather or suede to anteater, cobra, and eelskin, among others. His hats come in everything from the standard beaver to cool straw, and beautiful silver appears on just about everything.

For a few thousand dollars urban cowboys can sport this full-quill ostrich jacket (left). Fringed wrap skirt and pullover can be purchased in suede or deerskin (center). The bib-collar western shirt features silver buttons; both shirt and skirt are available in suede and deerskin (right). The women's shirts are also available for men.
(Courtesy of Preis-Grossman)

Stores like Laredo and its Parisian counterpart, El Paso Booty, also are beginning to feature American Indian styles, from fringed suedes to feather headdresses. If you'd like to see an example of the real extremes of the fashion, head for Nudie's, a western store in California's San Fernando Valley that is famous for outfitting the pro-western stars of Hollywood. Owner Nudleman himself is said to drive an outrageously flamboyant Cadillac, and his wares often reflect his taste. Customers can spend up to $2,000 for the utmost in western shirts, or a minimum of $1,000 for a single pair of boots.

For the in-between set, most of these western stores offer the Gary Cooper look offered by designers like Ralph Lauren, whose fashions can be seen in numerous print ads and in just about every department store you explore. In keeping with today's customers' desire for good-looking clothes that feel comfortable and look better as they get older, Lauren offers ruffled prairie skirts, fringed jackets, western shirts, and tweed jackets, among other garments.

Peggy Wright and Gator show how easy it is to do country dance steps.

CHAPTER 6

KICKIN' AND STOMPIN': COUNTRY DANCE STEPS

Hardly anyone could argue that country dance is a new form of recreation. Rather, it is an age-old diversion that has had its ups and downs throughout history, moving in and out of vogue with various people of different ages living in diverse communities. Teachers, historians, and dancers of all persuasions, however, have made sure that this important part of our dance history has not been lost to modern generations. Most adults can remember being taught a folk dance or two as schoolchildren, and many dance enthusiasts of all ages have joined country dance clubs in lieu of the Thursday night bowling team or the neighborhood bridge club.

The result of this, combined with country dance's origins in the rural and small-town segments of the world, is twofold: First, certain dances that spread quickly and widely across the continents can be learned in pretty much their original form by today's dancers. Second, the fact that they were danced by common folk, as opposed to the royal court dances of earlier centuries, laid them open to the whims of their current proponents. Thus, variations of every folk or country dance have come and gone, some destined to disappear with changing times and customs and others finding a permanent place in the culture of a community or an entire region.

One of the interesting things about folk dancing in general and cowboy dancing in particular is that it was created in rural areas and subsequently spread to urban communities, rather than the other way around. In today's world of urban glamor and sophisticated discos, country dancing provides a refreshing return to earlier, simpler ways. Today's country dances are being received with great enthusiasm in huge urban centers such as Los Angeles, Chicago, and New York, but most urbanites have little idea of how to do the dances and emulate the proper cowboy style.

Most of the dances included in this chapter have been recorded on paper somewhere in some form, but not to the extent that they are readily available to the average citizen. Further, it can be confusing to the newcomer who asks a few different country dancers to teach him or her a particular dance, only to find that the routines bear little resemblance to each other from one dancer to the other. Despite the spreading popularity of country dance in today's cities, written and illustrated instruction on these dances has not been available. And what began as a single dance now may be seen on the dance floor as many different routines that go under many different names.

Like folk dances of the past, even today's country dances have been in the background of people's lives in rural areas. Thus, these people often only had to relearn the dances rather than start from scratch. The amusing result of this, in dance halls like Gilley's, is that even the best dancers on the floor sometimes are hard pressed to actually describe the steps in the dances they do. And it is not easy for anyone to pick apart a dance in order to teach it to someone else. After all, dance is continuous motion, and when that motion is interrupted, it can be difficult to determine when one particular movement begins and the next ends, as well as which motions are made simultaneously, and what steps each partner must do. For this reason, we are indebted to Peggy Wright and Gator—two of the highest-steppers you'll ever see at the famous Gilley's—for taking the time and effort to dissect their favorite dances and pose for photographs of each step, so that we could bring them to you.

It is important to note that the dances in this chapter represent only one of many versions of each dance, and that they may go by different names according to the area of the U.S. you are in, and even the particular dance hall. The fact that we present only one version (with variations) of each dance here does not mean that these are *the* correct ways to do the dances. It simply means that, where country dance is concerned, different folks use different strokes, and as long as your style says "country," you won't feel out of place.

As explained in chapter 1, even the term "country dance" is but one of the many names used to refer to this style of dance. But whether you call it country, western, cowboy, or kicker dancing, it's got an unmistakable style of its own and cannot be confused with any form of disco dancing; contra, folk, or square dancing; or ballroom dancing. Traces of disco may appear in a cowboy dance hall, but they will be carefully cloaked under the name of "honky tonkin'" or sometimes known in a less enthusiastic form as "steppin' out." On the other hand, kicker dancing is creeping into many discos, but in this form it would hardly be considered the real thing by a bona fide urban cowboy.

Unlike disco dances, most of which are based on Latin and other dances of the 20th century, country dances done in dance halls like Gilley's stem from much older folk and peasant dances that originated in Europe. Naturally, these traditional dances have evolved quite a bit over the years. The schottische included here, for example, was a slow form of polka, the name coming from the German word for "Scottish." The polka also was once known as a Scotch waltz. Today the schottische has crossed the Atlantic to take on the characteristics of the cowboy style, and again even the name has been altered to reflect regional American cultures—in some locales, the schottische is spelled and pronounced shotess.

You will probably notice that the other dances in this chapter—the Texas Two-Step, polka, waltz, Cotton-Eyed Joe, Four Corners, and bunny hop—also recall traditional dances of the past. Other dances you might encounter include such classics as the crow's step, the whip, and the swing.

But regardless of what the dances are called and how they are performed, most urban cowboys will agree that they go to places like Gilley's as much or more for the total atmosphere of the place as for pure pursuit of dancing. In fact, an ignorant newcomer could follow the exact dance steps that the dance-hall regular uses and still look and feel out of place if he or she does not conform to the cowboy values and spirit that form the whole country dance scene.

Naturally, unspoken (but often rigid) rules for style and behavior will vary from dance hall to dance hall, but in general, the men are men and the women are girls in the world of the shit kicker. This may not sound very enlightened to a sophisticated urbanite, but that's the way it is at Gilley's and its counterparts, and this attitude definitely affects dance style. For instance, cowboy macho is evidenced in the fact that men always lead in partner dances. Men usually guard their hats the way the cowboys of old guarded their saddles, and no one takes off a hat while dancing. Even the couple's position on the dance floor sometimes smacks of female subservience: One of the most popular cowboy styles for slow dancing calls for the man to hold onto the woman's hair behind her back with his right hand, and for the woman to hook her left fingers into her partner's blue jean belt loops.

While dancers and spectators at western honky tonks are almost as likely to pay attention to style as are their disco counterparts, the nature of those two styles could not be further apart. While "style," as used by disco fans, could hardly be called subtle—and indeed is oriented toward grabbing the spotlight—the cowboy style in dance reflects the strong silent nature of the classic cowboy image. In the cowboy dance hall, silent tough replaces city slick, guts replace cool, and the way in which an urban cowboy sticks to the cowboy values and style is much more important than how many exotic acrobatics he or she can perform.

In pure dance terms, what is most important in pulling off country dancing is syncopation between partners, smoothness on the floor, and keeping time with the music—all the basic elements of good dancing with none of the flourishes that could be interpreted as exhibitionism, narcissism, and—heaven forbid—lack of manliness or womanliness.

The nature of the cowboy boot has dictated some of the modifications westerners have made to the basic country dances in this book. A cowboy dance is more likely to feature a flat-footed glide with some heel and toe touches added for flourish rather than a lot of toe-type dancing. Getting up on one's toes in those boots just isn't conducive to having a good time on the western dance floor.

Once kicker-dancers have mastered these basics, even the embellishments added to dances hark back to more traditional folk dance moves rather than to acrobatics and modern sensuality. Practiced dancers may add underarm turns to their dances, or classic promenades, or simple spins on the floor, sometimes dictated by a square dance type caller. There is no reason, of course, why you cannot use your own imagination in spicing up these dances; just be sure that you don't do anything that will make you stand out in a crowd of cowboys and cowgirls as a city slicker.

RULES FOR THE FLOOR

The following are some basic rules—or customs, if you will—applied to country dancing in most western-aura dance halls.

- The man usually dances forward.
- The woman usually dances backward.
- Couples usually dance counterclockwise around the outside of the floor.
- Beginners and those doing less straight-ahead routines should use the center of the floor to avoid collisions with those on the outside.

Syncopation and smoothness, rather than tricky footwork are hallmarks of country dancing.

DANCE POSITIONS

The positions of partners in a couples dance and those of singles in a line dance differ somewhat from the standard ballroom dance positions. Most of them recall the styles of early folk and country dances, and they often vary from dance hall to dance hall. You should, of course, use the position that feels most comfortable to you and your partner wherever a choice of positions is available. The following are some of the most common positions used in country dance.

OPEN POSITION.
This position is for couples and is used when a lively dance calls for extra space between partners. Facing each other, with about a foot of space between them, the man holds the woman's right hand in his left hand. The man extends his right arm to rest the right hand on the woman's left shoulder; the woman extends her left arm and rests her left hand on the man's right shoulder.

CLOSED POSITION.
Another couples position, this one is similar to the first but leaves just about no space between partners. It is often used for slower dances. The woman's right hand is held in the man's left. The man's right arm and the woman's left are circled around each other's waist so that each rests a hand on the partner's back.

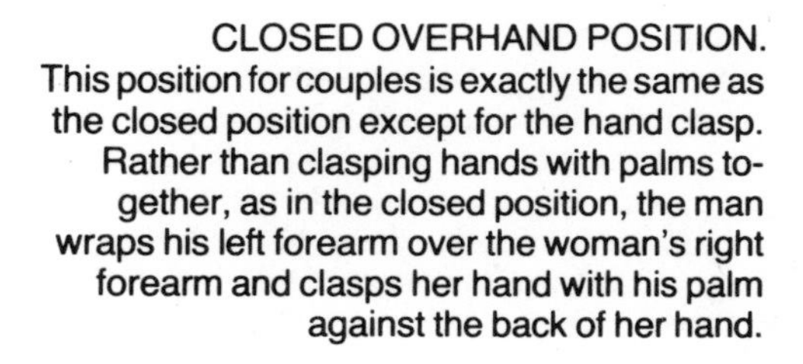

CLOSED OVERHAND POSITION.
This position for couples is exactly the same as the closed position except for the hand clasp. Rather than clasping hands with palms together, as in the closed position, the man wraps his left forearm over the woman's right forearm and clasps her hand with his palm against the back of her hand.

SIDE-BY-SIDE POSITION.
This position has been used for country and western-type folk dances for years and years. It is used by couples for lively dances in which both partners are going to travel around the floor dancing in the same direction and foot-stepping in tandem. Stand side by side and close together. In this version, the woman stands to the right of the man. The man's left wrist rests on his hip and the woman's left arm encircles his waist to clasp the man's left hand at his side. The man places his right across the woman's shoulders, and the woman bends her right elbow to clasp the man's right hand in front of her right shoulder.

ONE-HAND OPEN POSITION.
This jitterbug-type hold for couples is common in dance halls, though it is not used for any of the dances in this chapter. You may want to experiment with it in other country dances you learn. Facing each other, with plenty of space between partners, the woman holds her left arm loosely at her side and the man puts his left hand (or the back of his left wrist) on his hip. The woman's right hand and the man's right are clasped between them, with the elbows of those arms bent, the forearms held straight and parallel to the floor, and the upper arms held fairly close to the body. This hold is commonly used during spins or underarm turns within a dance that uses the open or closed couples positions.

LINE DANCE POSITIONS

Many different positions are used for various line and round dances, although the dancers normally do not come into contact with each other for any of them.

STRAIGHTFORWARD STANCE.
Probably the most common of the line dance positions is this straightforward stance in which the dancers merely stand side by side with feet parallel and arms hanging loosely at their sides.

SINGLE FILE.
Sometimes a dance calls for the participants to form a single file. In western dances, hands are often held on the hips.

BUNNY HOP.
This is the classic position for the bunny hop. Dancers line up in a single file, each with hands on the hips of the dancer in front. Naturally, the first person in line must put his or her hands on his or her own hips. You may notice that this is similar to the position used for many other dances in which the participants form a snaking sort of line on the floor, such as the conga.

COUNTRY DANCES

Once you have found a body position and hand clasp that feel comfortable to you, you are ready to try some of the foot-stompin', knee-slappin' routines that follow. Start with the first dance in the chapter—it is the simplest dance for beginners to perform well. Then you can progress through the other six dances, none of which is beyond the capabilities of a normally coordinated human being. Put on your hat and your boots, find a honky tonk, and join the cowboy fun!

TEXAS TWO-STEP

Try the Texas Two-Step before you attempt any of the other country dances in this chapter. It's the simplest dance to learn, just as the two-step is one of the first routines you probably would be taught at a ballroom dance class. After all, what could be easier than doing two steps?

The Texas Two-Step actually includes three steps—a quick step, a quick step, and then a slow step. The name of the dance, of course, refers to the two quick steps. Like the other dancers in this book, the version that follows is just one of the many two-steps you might see on the floor of a country dance hall or a formal ballroom. You might even recognize a two-step pattern being done by dancers who will call it something entirely different. Whatever the name of the actual series of steps, the two-step serves as a general-purpose dance that will get even the least coordinated couple through a country dance session looking like pros.

This straightforward dance can be adapted to music in either a 2/4 or a 4/4 meter. You can two-step to a variety of tempos, from a slow fox trot tune or ballad to a livelier country stomper. If you're just learning to dance, it is a good idea to begin with the slower numbers and move up to the quick music as your dancing improves. As in all country dances, the best effect is created when the dancers achieve a smooth gliding motion. Concentrate on keeping time with the music and on moving smoothly as a couple.

In the following photos, Gator and Peggy dance the Texas Two-Step in the closed position, although the open position or the closed overhand position can also be used.

STEP 1.
Start in the closed position. The couple will dance counterclockwise around the outside of the floor, with the man dancing forward and the woman dancing backward. To begin, Gator steps forward onto his left foot, lifting the right heel, as Peggy steps backward onto her right foot, lifting the left toe. Remember, this is the first quick step.

STEP 2.
This is another quick step. Gator steps forward onto his right foot, lifting the left heel, as Peggy steps backward onto her left foot, lifting the right toe.

STEP 3.
This step should be taken more slowly. Gator steps forward again onto his left foot, lifting the right heel, as Peggy steps backward onto her right foot, lifting the left toe.

To continue the two-step, just keep repeating the three steps—quick step, quick step, slow step—alternating feet and traveling counterclockwise around the floor. For the second series of three steps, the man does a quick step forward onto the right foot while the woman does a quick step backward onto her left foot. The next quick step is on the man's left foot and the woman's right foot, and the slow step is on the right foot for the man and the left foot for the woman.

This dance is so simple that enthusiasts will want to add their own personal style to jazz it up. Try adding a swaying body motion on the slow step in the series.

TEXAS TWO-STEP (ctd.)

VARIATIONS.
To break the monotony of the three steps (which bear a startling resemblance to a rhythmic walk) you can throw in a half turn or a full turn. Of course, as in all these dances, the male partner leads, so he must decide when to do a turn and cue his partner accordingly. The turns take a little more skill than the basic steps, but they are not difficult. The full turn is done on four steps, and the half turn on two. In the following photos, Gator and Peggy do a half turn as part of the two-step.

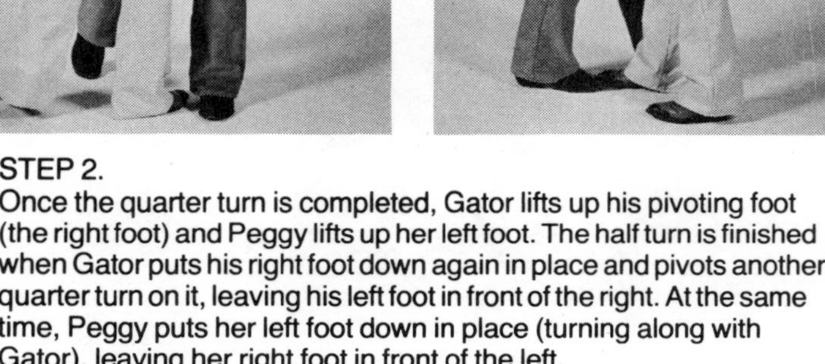

STEP 1.
Gator steps forward (quick step) onto his left foot while Peggy steps back onto her right foot, but this time the couple does a quarter turn counterclockwise (to Gator's left), which is achieved by Gator's pivoting on the ball of his right foot and turning Peggy along with him.

STEP 2.
Once the quarter turn is completed, Gator lifts up his pivoting foot (the right foot) and Peggy lifts up her left foot. The half turn is finished when Gator puts his right foot down again in place and pivots another quarter turn on it, leaving his left foot in front of the right. At the same time, Peggy puts her left foot down in place (turning along with Gator), leaving her right foot in front of the left.

A full turn is done by taking another two steps and doing two more quarter turns in the same direction to bring the couple back to their original position on the floor. The man steps forward onto his left foot as the woman steps backward onto her right. Then the man steps in place on his right foot and the woman steps in place on her left foot.

The two-step forms the basis for many other fancier dances. So once you have learned this version, you are ready to add extra moves to come up with new routines. For example, when you add a little hop to the basic Texas Two-Step, you can do the polka (see Pasadena Polka, p. 73).

PASADENA POLKA

The basic polka is one of the oldest and most widespread of folk dances, and many versions of it have evolved over the decades. The variation of this lively dance described below is the polka done at Gilley's of Pasadena, Texas. This is also an easy dance to do, but it's not for the faint-hearted. All polkas call for a lot of energy and bounce.

The Pasadena Polka is danced to a 2/4 meter, and the dance steps form an uneven, springy rhythm. The speed of the polka can vary, although it's usually the songs with a lively beat that draw polka fans out onto the floor. Again, it's a good idea to try medium-tempo tunes when you're learning the dance. As soon as you feel confident in knowing the steps, you will undoubtedly want to polka faster and faster for the sheer fun of it. However, keep in mind that the faster you move and the harder you stomp, the more likely it is that you'll hurt someone if you don't watch out for other couples and the feet of your own partner. If you want to dance faster or slower than the speed of the general crowd, it's a good idea to head for the center of the floor and stay out of everyone's way.

In the following photos, Gator and Peggy dance the polka in the open position, but the dance also can be done in the side-by-side position. Note that if you polka side by side, both partners will do the steps in the same direction on the same feet. Basically, the polka is six steps, or two series of three steps each. The second series of three steps is merely a repeat of the first three, but on the opposite feet. Concentrate on making your steps bouncy but not heavy-footed—and count on having to take a breather when the polka is over.

STEP 1.
Starting in the open position, Gator steps forward onto his left foot, bending the right knee and lifting the right heel high off the floor, as Peggy steps back onto her right foot, lifting her left toe high.

STEP 2.
Now Gator brings his right foot forward so that it is just behind the left foot, putting only the ball of the right foot on the floor. At the same time, Peggy brings her left foot backward so that it is just in front of her right foot, stepping on the ball of her left foot. Gator's left foot and Peggy's right foot stay flat on the floor.

PASADENA POLKA (ctd.)

STEP 3.
Do this step quickly and lightly. Gator rocks back on the ball of his right foot, then lifts the left foot and steps forward onto it as he rocks forward. Peggy rocks forward on the ball of her left foot and then lifts the right foot and steps backward onto it as she rocks backward.

STEP 4.
Next, Gator takes a step forward onto his right foot, bending the left knee and lifting the left heel high off the floor, as Peggy steps backward onto her left foot, lifting her right toe high. Note that this is exactly like step 1, but the dancers use the opposite feet.

STEP 5.
This is the same move as step 2 but on opposite feet. Gator brings his left foot forward so that it is just behind the right foot, putting only the ball of the left foot on the floor, as Peggy brings her right foot back so that it is just in front of her left foot, putting only the ball of the right foot down. Gator's right foot and Peggy's left stay on the floor.

STEP 6.
Now, as in step 3, Gator rocks back on the ball of his left foot, then lifts his right foot and steps forward onto it as he rocks forward. Peggy rocks forward on the ball of her right foot, then lifts her left foot and steps backward onto it as she rocks backward.

Continue dancing these six steps as you polka counterclockwise around the floor. For interest, try the following variations.

VARIATIONS.
To do the polka side by side, both partners do the man's steps and dance in the same direction.

You can also add a half turn or a full turn to the Pasadena Polka. A half turn is done on three steps and a full turn on six; the couple turns counterclockwise. The following photos show how to insert a half turn into the polka.

STEP 1.
As in the basic steps, Gator begins the turn by stepping forward onto his left foot but with a counterclockwise quarter turn on this step. Peggy steps backward onto her right foot, turning along with Gator.

STEP 2.
Now Gator brings his right foot up behind the left foot, resting only on the ball of the right foot, as Peggy brings her left foot back in front of the right foot, and they pivot on those feet to complete the first quarter turn.

STEP 3.
To complete the pivot and the half turn, Gator steps out and forward again on his left foot as Peggy steps back in place onto her right foot.

WALTZ

Waltzes come in a multitude of varieties and styles, from the very beautiful Skater's Waltz and Spanish Circle Waltz to the Penny Waltz and the Black Hawk Waltz. Waltzes originated in Europe and came to this country as very formal and proper dances for ballrooms. However, because of the versatility of the waltz and its easy adaptation to slow, medium, and fast tempos, the waltz became a natural part of the country dance repertoire.

The cowboy version of the waltz is a bit different from the classic version. Rather than consisting of a gliding step followed by two quick steps on the balls of the dancer's feet, this waltz is suited to dancing in cowboy boots and consists of all gliding steps in which neither foot is ever lifted completely off the floor. The steps could hardly be simpler to do; the only trick is in keeping time with the music, which is always in 3/4 time.

Think of each step as a glide in which your foot slides across the floor with grace and a smooth swaying motion of the body. Use the standard waltz position that Peggy and Gator use.

If you're used to dancing to the more common 4/4 and 2/4 time songs, you may have a little difficulty adjusting to 3/4 time, so we'll review the correlation between the music's beat and the dancer's steps to make things easier. First of all, remember that you will be counting 1, 2, 3; 1, 2, 3 during the waltz, instead of 1, 2, 3, 4; 1, 2, 3, 4 or 1, 2; 1, 2. If you are familiar with the classic waltz, you know that you take three steps for every three beats. But in our version of the waltz, this pattern is different: The first two steps are done together to three beats of music; the second two steps combined are done to three beats; steps 5 and 6 are *each* done to a full three beats.

STEP 1.
This step is done to one beat of music. Gator slides his left foot forward and slightly to the left, lifting his right heel, as Peggy slides her right foot back and to the right, lifting her left toe.

STEP 2.
This step takes up two beats. Gator slides his right foot forward on the ball of the foot so that its toe is adjacent to the left heel and hesitates (for that second beat) in this position. At the same time, Peggy brings her left foot back so that its toe is adjacent to her right heel, then hesitates for one beat.

STEP 3.
Do this move on one beat. Gator's right foot slides forward and to the right a little, and his left heel comes off the floor, as Peggy's left foot slides backward and to the left and her right toe comes off the floor.

STEP 4.
Again, this step takes two beats. The move is the same as step 2 but with opposite feet. Gator slides his left foot forward on the ball of the foot, bringing its toe up to the right heel, as Peggy slides her right foot back so that its toe is adjacent to her left heel. The couple hesitates in this position for the second beat.

STEP 5.
On three full beats of music, the dancers repeat step 1.

STEP 6.
On another three beats, the dancers repeat step 3.

At this point, having completed all six steps, you should have gone through four full measures of three beats each. To review the pattern: step 1 (beat 1), step 2 (beats 2 and 3), step 3 (beat 1), step 4 (beats 2 and 3), step 5 (beats 1, 2, and 3), and step 6 (beats 1, 2, and 3). Now you can begin the whole series again, traveling counterclockwise around the floor until the music ends.

Note that the waltz will not look its best unless you remember to glide along the balls of your feet throughout the dance. Remember, there's a big difference between a light-footed glide and a flat-footed shuffle.

SCHOTTISCHE

This old European folk dance that resembles a polka has been subject to many modern alterations and embellishments. When the name schottische is used, it usually refers to the classic sequence of steps that ends in a hop. Even this has changed over the years, bringing us countless versions of the popular dance. In fact, in Texas alone, you might see people doing schottische-type dances that go by the names of Drunk, Blue Bonnet, McGinty, and Douglas—all on the same floor at the same time.

Like many folk-country dances, the schottische is always lively but should be danced smoothly and evenly. The steps are quite simple—there are only four steps to learn—and the dance is usually done to music in 4/4 time. Originally a round dance, it can be adapted by modern kickers to a round dance, a line dance, or a couples dance. Whichever way it is executed, the dancers all face the same direction and do the steps on the same feet.

Today the schottische probably is done more frequently as a partner dance, if for no other reason than that it's not so easy to gather a large group at once for a line or round version. The following rendition of the schottische is that done at Gilley's. In the photos below, Gator and Peggy use the standard side-by-side position.

STEP 1.
Step forward and a little to the left on the left foot. Note that this step is most effective when the dancers jut their left hips out to the side, as Gator does in the photo.

STEP 2.
Now cross your right foot behind the left foot, keeping the legs relatively straight for a smooth, clean line.

STEP 3.
Next, uncross your legs by swinging your left foot back to the left and across the right foot, moving to the left and forward a little on the floor.

STEP 4.
Now swing your right leg out and up in a straight-leg kick to the left.

STEP 5. (Not shown)
Return your right foot to the floor by stepping forward and to the right on your right foot.

STEP 6.
Now cross your left foot behind your right foot, to the right side, keeping your legs straight.

STEP 7.
Again uncross your legs by swinging your right foot across the left, to the right side, and forward a little.

STEP 8.
Finally, do another straight-leg kick but with the left leg, kicking to the right side.

Steps 5-8 are just steps 1-4 done on the opposite feet and moving to the right on the floor instead of to the left.

SCHOTTISCHE (ctd.)

Repeat the entire eight-step pattern until the music ends. Once you have mastered this simple sequence, you might want to try inserting some of the variations described below.

VARIATIONS.
On steps 4 and 8, you may substitute either of the following moves for the straight-leg kick. Both include the traditional hop that is part of the original schottische.

KICK-HOP.
You can try a kick-hop by lifting the leg up for a bent-knee kick, hopping off the standing foot at the same time.

STANDING HOP.
If you prefer, try the standing hop on steps 4 and 8. Without kicking the leg forward, just bend the knee and lift the foot, keeping it close to the other leg, hopping in this position at the same time.

FOUR CORNERS

This is a great old-style dance that is usually done as a line dance by a large group of solo kickers. It can, of course, be danced by a couple, but the Four Corners most commonly serves as a great dance hall icebreaker for singles.

This dance is light, bouncy, and a lot of fun, especially when the challenge of staying in time with a large group is added. Just about any type and tempo of music will serve, but a medium-tempo tune might be best for a large group.

Those who know disco dancing may be familiar with the concept of Four Corners and other similar line dances. The title of the dance refers to the fact that the whole line of kickers does the entire sixteen-step routine in each of four directions. In other words, after completing the sixteen steps, the dancers turn a "corner" by turning 90 degrees (a quarter turn), and then go through the sixteen steps again in the new direction. The pattern is thus completed four full times facing, for example, south, east, north, and west, or forward, to the left, backward, and to the right. The dancers end the routine facing in the starting direction.

Whether you do the Four Corners with a partner or a whole mob, dancers begin by standing side by side without touching each other. Your feet should be close together and parallel, and your arms held loosely at your side. In the photos that follow, Peggy starts out standing to Gator's right side.

FIRST CORNER.

STEP 1.
Spread your heels apart.

STEP 2.
Now put your heels back in the original position so that your feet are parallel.

STEP 3.
Leaving your left foot on the floor, put your right foot forward, heel on the floor and toe raised; at the same time, put your hands on your hips. Your hands will stay on your hips throughout the rest of the sixteen steps.

STEP 4.
Now cross your right foot over the left (to the left side), leaving your weight on the left foot and touching the right toe to the floor.

STEP 5.
Now swing your right foot back across the left foot (to the right) and touch your right heel in front.

STEP 6.
Next, bring your right foot back so that it is close to and parallel to the left foot, as in step 2.

STEP 7.
Touch your left heel to the floor in front and slightly to the left side.

STEP 8.
Now cross your left foot over the right foot (to the right side) and touch your left toe to the right side.

STEP 9.
Swing your left foot back over the right foot and touch the left heel to the front and slightly to the left side.

STEP 10.
Next, bring your left foot back so that it is close to and parallel to the right foot, as in step 2.

STEP 11.
Step forward onto your left foot, leaving the toe of the right foot on the floor.

STEP 12.
Now step forward onto your right foot, leaving your left foot on the floor. Note that you may put only your right heel on the floor, leaving the right toe raised if you wish, as Peggy does in this photo.

STEP 13.
Step backward onto your right foot.

STEP 14.
Bring your left foot back to the right foot, so that your feet are close together and parallel.

STEP 15.
Now step forward onto your left foot.

STEP 16.
For the final step in the first "corner," swing your right foot over and around the left foot, at the same time pivoting counter-clockwise 90 degrees (a quarter turn) on the left foot. You have now turned one of the four corners. Note that this puts Peggy behind Gator.

FOUR CORNERS (ctd.)

SECOND CORNER.
The entire line is now in a column with the dancers facing each other's backs, and you're ready to start the whole sixteen-step sequence again. Begin with step 1 by bringing your left foot up to the right foot and then spreading your heels. Complete the remaining steps, turning another corner on step 16. Now the dancers will be facing the exact opposite direction from the beginning of the dance, and in these photos Peggy would be to Gator's left side.

THIRD CORNER.
In this new direction (a half turn from your original position), all sixteen steps are completed again. You then turn another corner—90 degrees counterclockwise—to put all the dancers facing in a new direction. The dancers will be in a column again, and Peggy would be in front of Gator.

FOURTH CORNER.
Facing in this direction, complete the sixteen-step sequence again, ending with a final turn that puts the dancers back in their original position and direction on the floor. In other words, Peggy would again be to Gator's right side. Depending on the custom in your local dance hall, and on the length of the musical number you dance to, the group may wish to complete the sixteen steps a fifth time, repeating the exact sequence of steps in the same direction as in the first corner.

This is the floor pattern followed by a single dancer completing the entire Four Corners:

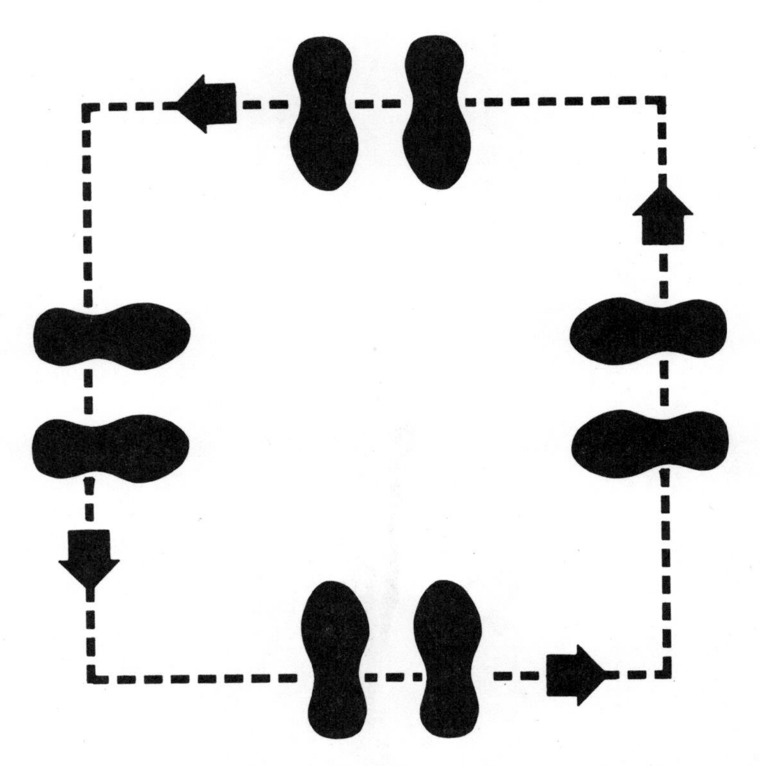

THE FOUR CORNERS FOOT PATTERN

COTTON-EYED JOE

This is one of the favorites of country and cowboy dances. Whenever the fiddler strikes up that old slave tune, "Cotton-Eyed Joe," the floor fills up with lines of kickers joyously dancing their version of this traditional routine.

The Cotton-Eyed Joe has the flair of a polka, and at places like Gilley's it can be rather rowdy. This dance is for true shit kickers. At Gilley's the caller will yell, "What did ya step in?" at precisely the right moment for all the dancers to shout back, "Bullshit! Bullshit!" on the swing kick step in the dance.

Danced to a good ol' country tune that goes by the same name, the Cotton-Eyed Joe has a strong beat, though the tempo may vary from caller to caller and from dance hall to dance hall. Sixteen steps form our version of this timeless stomp. As in the photos that follow, the dancers use the side-by-side position, so everyone does the same steps with the same feet.

STEP 1.
Step forward onto your left foot.

STEP 2.
Now bring your right foot forward, crossing it behind the left foot to the left side, putting only the ball of the right foot on the floor.

STEP 3.
Next, rock back onto the ball of your right foot and step forward onto the left foot again.

STEP 4.
Step forward onto the right foot.

STEP 5.
Now bring your left foot forward, crossing it behind the right foot to the right side, putting only the ball of the left foot on the floor.

STEP 6.
Rock back onto the ball of the left foot and step forward onto the right foot again.

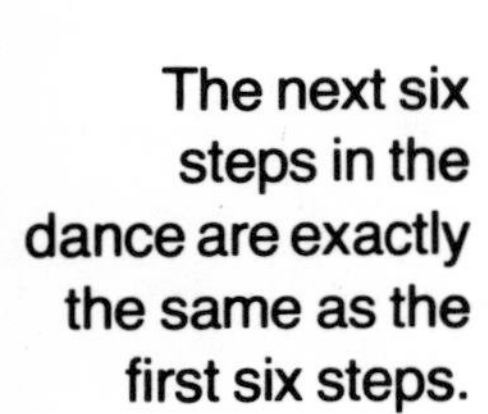

The next six steps in the dance are exactly the same as the first six steps.

STEP 7.
Step forward onto your left foot.

STEP 8.
Now bring the right foot forward to cross behind the left foot.

STEP 9.
Rock back onto the right foot and step forward onto the left foot.

STEP 10.
Now step forward onto the right foot.

STEP 11.
Now bring your left foot forward to cross behind the right foot.

STEP 12.
Rock back onto the left foot and step forward onto the right foot.

STEP 13.
Now bring your left foot over and around the front of your right foot, bending your left knee and pointing the left toe toward the floor to the right side of the standing (right) foot.

Then quickly kick the left foot shortly and sharply forward and to the left as if you were shaking something off the bottom of your foot, returning the kicking foot to the floor. This kick is the step on which the crowd yells, "Bullshit!" in answer to the caller.

STEP 14.
Next, step backward onto your right foot.

STEP 15.
Now step backward onto your left foot.

STEP 16.
Now swing your right foot over the front of the left foot, to the left side of the left foot, then kick it out sharply forward and to the right as in step 13, but do this kick four times here.

At this point, you will have progressed farther forward than backward, so in short order you should be making your way around the dance floor. The real trick is in keeping everyone in step, taking the same-length steps so that no one ends up in a tangle on the floor.

After you have completed the four right-foot kicks and returned your right foot to the floor, you are ready to begin the entire series again, starting with step 1.

If you dance the Cotton-Eyed Joe with a partner, rather than as a single in a line dance, you can add the following turn to the routine. This, however, is really only for experienced dancers.

OVERHEAD TURN.
This turn is a little easier than it looks and a lot more fun to do. It should be done very smoothly, so don't let the stop-action photos fool you. You might even learn this turn more quickly if you try only the arm movements first. Once you understand how the arms are looped over the head in a smooth motion, you'll be able to add the steps. This is done on eight steps, but it includes a lot more movements than the steps in the basic Cotton-Eyed Joe.

STEP 1.
Starting side by side as earlier, the couple breaks the clasp of the left hands during this step. Gator leaves his left hand on his hip and Peggy drops hers. Gator steps forward and pivots to his right on his left foot, as Peggy makes a half turn to her left by a step and pivot on her left foot.

STEP 2.
To bring them into the side-by-side position again, Peggy pivots to her left again by bringing her right foot up to the left foot, as Gator brings his right foot up to his left foot.

STEP 3.
Both partners rock back on their right feet and join left hands again as Gator begins to lift his right arm over Peggy's head. Then Gator loops his right arm all the way over Peggy's head as he steps forward and around his right foot onto his left; Peggy does the same move in the opposite direction onto her right foot. Note that during this whole step Peggy and Gator extend their clasped arms out to the side after they are looped over Peggy's head.

STEP 4.
From this step to the end of the turn, the dancers do the steps on opposite feet. Gator uncrosses his legs by bringing his right foot around the left foot and stepping forward on his right foot, as Peggy brings her left foot over and around her right foot, stepping forward on the left foot. During this step, Gator loops his left arm over and behind Peggy's head. While Gator is bringing his arm behind Peggy she takes a quick step with her right foot to bring them back to even feet.

STEP 5.
To bring the couple back to their original position in which right hands are clasped in front of Peggy's shoulder and left hands are ready to clasp behind Gator's back and at his waist, Peggy moves in front of Gator by stepping out onto her left foot.

STEP 6.
Then Gator steps to the left and forward (crossing behind Peggy) as Peggy steps forward on her right foot.

STEP 7.
Then Peggy steps backward onto her left foot, pivoting counterclockwise to leave her right foot in front of the left, as Gator steps toward her on his right foot.

STEP 8.
Peggy now steps backward and pivots in the same direction onto the right foot. Peggy takes a final pivoting step onto her left foot as Gator is stepping forward on his right foot.

As shown in the photos, during steps 5 through 7, the dancers clasped right hands are looped over Peggy's head once again. On Peggy's last two steps, the clasp of the left hands is broken. Now Peggy and Gator are standing in the same position as they were in before the turn was done, and they may reclasp left hands behind Gator's back to begin the basic Cotton-Eyed Joe again.

BUNNY HOP

If you grew up in the United States, you probably learned the bunny hop at one time or another. And for all of you who thought that this dance was just for kids, remember that kids come in all ages. Truly, this dance can be a lot of fun it you're up for a few giggles and a lot of bouncing off the floor.

This is usually danced to the standard "bunny hop" tune, in 4/4 time. In case you don't recall, it's a line dance in which the participants line up one behind the other, with hands on the hips of the person in front. Let's hop!

STEP 1.
On cue, so that everyone starts together, kick your left foot out to touch the heel on the floor in front of you and slightly to the left.

STEP 2.
Now kick your left foot forward again but higher and with some snap this time.

STEP 3.
Now repeat step 1 with the right foot.

STEP 4.
Repeat step 2, but use the right foot.

STEP 5.
Bring your feet together and take one hop forward.

STEP 6.
Take one hop backward.

STEPS 7-9.
Take three more hops forward.

Begin again with step 1, and continue the whole series until the song ends. There are usually no variations to this dance, since it is well known and commonly done in its original form.

INDEX